Bible Exploration for High School
A Two-Year Course

Student Workbook
Year 2

Ron Cohen

Brilliant Jewel Press

Bible Exploration for High School
Student Workbook—Year 2

Copyright © 2015 Brilliant Jewel Press
All rights reserved.

Scripture quotations are taken from the New American Standard Bible®,
Copyright © 1960, 1962, 1963, 1968, 1971, 1972, 1973, 1975, 1977, 1995 by The Lockman
Foundation. Used by permission. (www.Lockman.org).

Scripture quotations marked (NLT) are taken from the *Holy Bible*, New Living Translation,
copyright © 1996, 2004, 2007 by Tyndale House Foundation. Used by permission of
Tyndale House Publishers, Inc., Carol Stream, Illinois 60188. All rights reserved.

Scripture quotations marked (KJV) are from the King James Version.

Reproduction or translation of any part of this work beyond that permitted by Section 107
and 108 of the 1976 United States Copyright Act without the written permission of the
copyright owner is unlawful. Requests for permission or other information must be secured
from the publisher.

Brilliant Jewel Press
24896 Deep Well Road
Wildomar, CA 92595
brilliantjewelpress@gmail.com

(Student workbooks with coil bindings, which open flat, can be ordered from either address.)

Printed in the United States of America.

ISBN: 978-0-69238-486-2   Paperback
       978-1-63315-889-4   CD

Table of Contents

Semester 1
Activities

1. **Presentation:** Prepare a multi-chart (or computer-based) presentation showing the early combined kingdom and the later divided kingdoms. How were they similar to each other and how were they different? What factors contributed to the rise and fall of each? What were their relationships to neighboring nations? What lessons can be learned?

2. **Skit:** Write a skit about the life of Hosea. Present it to your youth group at church.

3. **Epistle:** Assume you are the Apostle Paul and write a letter (or epistle) to your own church.

4. **Psalm:** Write your own psalm, poem, or song about the attributes of God and what God has done for you.

5. **Report:** What evidence is there to support the bodily resurrection of Jesus? Investigate events and eyewitnesses. Is the evidence compelling? What are the implications for mankind? Prepare a written report. See 1 Corinthians 15.

Essays

1. Elisha asked Elijah for a "double portion" (2 Kings 2:9). Compare and contrast events in the lives of Elijah and Elisha that support the fulfillment of this request.

2. What were the root causes for the division of the kingdom into two? What were the reasons the kingdom of Judah remained intact far longer than the kingdom of Israel?

3. Discuss the impact that Isaiah had upon Hezekiah's life (see 2 Kings 18–20, 2 Chronicles 29–32, Isaiah 36–39).

4. The book of Isaiah provides many prophetic pictures of various aspects of the life and ministry of the Messiah. Which passage(s) impress you? Which passage(s) touch your heart? Describe their impact upon you.

5. Provide details from John the Baptist's ministry to support how he fulfilled the prophecies of Isaiah 40:3 and Malachi 3:1. With regards to his being Elijah (see Malachi 4:5–6), can John the Baptist's statements and Jesus' statements be reconciled? Support your answer.

6. Compare both the parable of the landowner and the hostile tenants and the parable of the wedding banquet (Matthew 21:33–22:14) to the history of Israel through their captivity.

7. Discuss major issues addressed in 1 Corinthians and Paul's instructions for handling them. How relevant are these issues to today?

8. Describe Paul's defense of his ministry in 2 Corinthians 10–13. How do you think this was received by his detractors in Corinth? If you could, is there anything you would add to his defense?

Unit 1 Divided Kingdom

1. In his prayer, what four things did Jabez ask of God?

   _____

   _____

   _____

   _____

2. Why was the birthright of Jacob's sons transferred from Reuben to Joseph's sons?

   _____

3. What did the tribe of Reuben, the tribe of Gad, and the half-tribe of Manasseh do to become the first of Israel to be deported into Assyrian captivity?

   _____

   _____

4. What was the advice of the elders to Rehoboam?

   _____

   _____

   What was the advice of the young men who grew up with him?

   _____

   _____

   Whose advice did he follow?

   _____

What were the consequences?

_____

_____

5. Why did the priests, Levites, and those from the tribes of Israel who were God-seekers, move from Israel to Judah and Jerusalem?

_____

_____

_____

6. What happened to Jeroboam when he threatened the man of God?

_____

What did Jeroboam do next?

_____

_____

How did the man of God respond?

_____

_____

What was the result?

_____

7. What were the consequences to the man of God who believed the lie from the old prophet and acted upon it?

_____

_____

_____

8. How did Jeroboam try to fool Ahijah the prophet?

_____

_____

How did Ahijah learn of this deception?

_____

_____

What was Ahijah's message to her?

_____

_____

_____

9. Why did Rehoboam replace the shields of gold which Solomon had made with shields of bronze?

_____

_____

10. What was the strategy of Asa (king of Judah) in the civil war against Baasha (king of Israel)?

_____

_____

What was the flaw in this strategy?

_____

_____

11. At the end of his life, how did Asa fail the LORD with regards to a severe disease in his feet?

_____

_____

_____

Unit 2 Elijah and Elisha

1. Compare 1 Kings 17:3 with 1 Kings 19:3.

_____

_____

_____

_____

2. What did the Zarephathian widow have to do in order for the LORD to give her miraculous provisions?

_____

_____

_____

3. What was Elijah's challenge to the people at Mount Carmel?

_____

_____

    How did Elijah mock the prophets of Baal?

_____

_____

How did the LORD support Elijah?

_____

_____

_____

4. Elijah traveled to Mount Horeb (Mount Sinai) and God spoke to him there (1 Kings 19:8–18). Much earlier in Israel's history, God spoke to another man from Mount Horeb—who was he?

_____

These two men together met Jesus during His ministry—where was this?

_____

5. Who became Elijah's successor?

_____

What was he doing when Elijah met him?

_____

What did he do to show he was moving on to a new career?

_____

_____

6. What was Elisha's last request of Elijah?

_____

_____

What did Elijah tell Elisha he needed to do to assure this would happen?

_____

_____

How did Elijah die?

_____

_____

_____

7. List three miracles that were common to both Elijah and Elisha.

_____

_____

_____

_____

8. List the similarities between 2 Kings 4:42–44 and John 6:1–13.

_____

_____

_____

_____

9. What did Naaman have to do to be healed of leprosy?

_____

_____

What did Gehazi do that caused him to be afflicted with leprosy?

_____

_____

_____

10. Why did the king of Aram want to kidnap Elisha?

_____

_____

   How did Elisha spoil this plot?

_____

_____

_____

_____

11. What were the first two things Jehoshaphat did when he was confronted by the Moabites, the Ammonites, and the Meunites?

_____

_____

   Whom did he send out before (in front of) the army?

_____

12. Psalm 80 includes many metaphors that Jesus later used to refer to Himself. List these metaphors.

_____

_____

_____

_____

Unit 3 1 Corinthians

1. What was the first set of problems in the Corinthian church that Paul addressed?

_____

_____

2. Paul contrasted the Jews to the Greeks/non-Jews. The Jews ask for

_____ ; the preaching of Christ crucified is _____

_____ to the Jews; Christ is _____

_____ to the Jews who are called. The Greeks/non-Jews

search for _____ ; the preaching of Christ crucified is

_____ to the Greeks/non-Jews; Christ is

_____ to the Greeks/non-Jews

who are called.

3. Why are believers to avoid suing one another in secular courts?

_____

_____

_____

   Compare 1 Corinthians 6:7 with Matthew 5:40.

_____

_____

_____

4. List four reasons why we are to run from sexual immorality.

_____

_____

_____

_____

5. When is eating food sacrificed to idols a sin?

_____

_____

_____

6. What two ways will God help each of us to deal with temptation?

_____

_____

_____

7. What is the reason for taking part in the Lord's Supper?

_____

_____

   To prepare for taking part in the Lord's Supper, what is each person to do?

_____

_____

8. List the nine manifestation gifts, which the Spirit distributes "to each one individually just as He wills."

_____

_____

_____

_____

_____

_____

What is God's purpose for these gifts?

_____

_____

What motive is key to moving in the manifestation gifts?

_____

9. List the attributes of love.

_____

_____

_____

_____

_____

_____

10. Who were the eyewitnesses to the resurrected Jesus listed by Paul?

_____

_____

_____

_____

What does it mean if there is no resurrection of the dead (as some of the Corinthians had claimed)?

_____

_____

_____

_____

_____

11. Compare Adam to Jesus.

_____

_____

_____

_____

_____

12. What is the mystery regarding our bodies "at the last trumpet"?

_____

_____

_____

What is the victory for those who have taken Jesus Christ as Lord?

_____

_____

How are we to act now in response?

_____

_____

_____

_____

Unit 4 Kingdom of Israel Falls

1. When Athaliah stole the throne of Judah after her son the king died, what woman saved the life of one of the royal offspring?

    _____

    _____

    Where was the boy hidden and for how long was he hidden?

    _____

    _____

    What happened afterward?

    _____

    _____

    _____

    _____

2. How were the bow and arrows of the king of Israel linked symbolically to Elisha's prophecy?

_____

_____

_____

_____

Why did Elisha become angry with the king?

_____

_____

_____

3. What miracle occurred involving Elisha's dead body?

_____

_____

4. Why did King Uzziah become leprous?

_____

_____

_____

5. Why was Israel ultimately deported to Assyria?

_____

_____

_____

6. What happened to some of the people who resettled in Samaria?

_____

_____

What was the king of Assyria's response?

_____

_____

Did this work? Why or why not?

_____

_____

_____

7. From Acts 2, in his sermon on the Day of Pentecost, the Apostle Peter quoted

from Joel 2:28–32 to describe the outpouring of _____ .

8. From Amos, what was the significance of the plumb line?

_____

_____

_____

9. From Obadiah, the deliverers who would ascend Mount Zion and judge Esau/Edom were symbolic of whom?

_____

10. From Jonah, what miracle caused the sailors to worship the LORD?

_____

_____

11. In his own words, Jonah told the LORD that he fled from His calling at first for what reason?

_____

_____

_____

_____

12. While tempting Jesus in the wilderness, the devil quoted from Psalm 91:11–12, but removed what key phrase?

_____

_____

Describe how the meaning of this passage changes with the removal of this key phrase.

_____

_____

_____

_____

_____

Unit 5 Kingdom of Judah Falls

1. Why did King Hezekiah smash up the bronze serpent that Moses had made?

_____

_____

2. When mortally ill, what did Hezekiah do upon hearing Isaiah's prophecy for him?

_____

_____

What was Isaiah's prophecy in response?

_____

_____

What was the miracle that the LORD performed as a sign that He would heal Hezekiah?

_____

_____

3. How did King Manasseh defile the temple?

_____

_____

What was Manasseh's influence upon the people of Judah?

_____

_____

4. When Manasseh failed to listen to the LORD, what tragedy befell Manasseh personally?

_____

_____

What was Manasseh's response?

_____

_____

What was the LORD's response?

_____

_____

How did Manasseh demonstrate his change of heart?

_____

_____

_____

5. During King Josiah's reign, what important object was found during the temple repairs?

_____

_____

What was the prophetess Huldah's prophecy?

_____

_____

What did King Josiah do next?

_____

_____

_____

6. Why were the people of Judah deported to Babylon?

_____

_____

_____

How long were they held in captivity?

_____

Who ordered their return to the land of Judah?

_____

7. What kind of woman did God tell Hosea to marry?

_____

Why?

_____

_____

8. What were the names of Hosea's three children? What was the significance of each name?

_____

_____

_____

_____

9. How did Hosea later get his wife back (from prostitution and slavery)?

_____

_____

What did Hosea then require of her?

_____

_____

To what was this act symbolic?

_____

_____

10. Explain the meaning of the following message: "I gave you a king in My anger and took him away in My wrath (Hosea 13:11)."

_____

_____

_____

_____

Unit 6 2 Corinthians

1. What was Paul's instruction for the man who had been punished by the church body?

_____

_____

_____

2. The Lord gave us _____ as a pledge. The Greek word for "pledge" can be translated as "down payment." What is the total promise from God that this down payment guarantees?

_____

_____

3. Where must all of us one day appear?

_____

_____

Therefore, what should be our goal here on earth?

_____

_____

4. What is our key responsibility as ambassadors of Christ?

_____

_____

5. What is the major reason that a believer is not to marry (be bound together with) an unbeliever?

_____

_____

_____

6. What is the difference between the sorrow that is according to God's will and the sorrow of the world?

_____

_____

_____

7. List the examples Paul used to show the grace of God to the Macedonian churches.

_____

_____

_____

_____

8. What arguments did Paul use to convince the Corinthians to complete the work started by the Macedonian churches?

_____

_____

_____

_____

9. What is to be our attitude in giving?

_____

_____

What attitudes are we to avoid?

_____

_____

10. What are we to do with each and every thought?

_____

_____

11. Besides the many physical and personal attacks that Paul had suffered, what caused him ongoing stress?

_____

_____

12. Why was Paul given a "thorn in the flesh"?

_____

_____

What does Paul specifically say the thorn in the flesh was?

_____

How did Paul respond to it?

_____

_____

What was the Lord's reply?

_____

_____

What was the lesson that Paul learned?

_____

_____

_____

Unit 7 Isaiah, Part 1

1. Isaiah's ministry spanned the reigns of which four kings of Judah?

_____

_____

2. The LORD told Isaiah that He has had enough of what?

_____

_____

What does the LORD want of His people?

_____

_____

_____

Explain the meaning of the LORD's request: "Come now, and let us reason together."

_____

_____

_____

3. In the year of King Uzziah's death, Isaiah had a vision of heaven. Whom did he see?

_____

How did Isaiah respond?

_____

_____

How was this remedied?

_____

_____

What, then, did the LORD ask?

_____

_____

How did Isaiah respond?

_____

_____

To whom do you think the "Us" refers?

_____

_____

4. List the names for the Messiah found in Isaiah 7, 9, and 12.

_____

_____

_____

_____

5. Isaiah 9:1–4 is a prophecy concerning the future of Galilee—to what activity in the New Testament does this refer?

_____

_____

_____

6. Isaiah 14:12–15 refers to Lucifer ("star of the morning") who is now Satan. What was his sin?

_____

_____

_____

7. From Isaiah 27:8–9, what two removals made up the full price of pardoning Jacob's (Israel's) sin?

_____

_____

_____

8. In 1 Corinthians 14:21, the Apostle Paul quoted from Isaiah 28:11 in relation to what spiritual gift?

_____

_____

9. In 1 Peter 2:4–8, the Apostle Peter quoted from Isaiah 28:16—Jesus Christ is

a _____ and _____ corner stone, the foundation of a spiritual house, built up with believers, who all, like Jesus,

are _____ stones.

10. Isaiah 35 is a prophecy about the Second Coming of Christ. It lists what blessings for the redeemed?

_____

_____

_____

_____

11. From Psalm 103, we are charged to "forget none of His benefits." Provide a list of His benefits.

_____

_____

_____

_____

_____

_____

_____

_____

Unit 8 Isaiah, Part 2

1. Isaiah 40:3 is a prophecy that was fulfilled in the New Testament by whom?

_____

2. How is the word of God contrasted to the grass?

_____

_____

What does the grass represent?

_____

_____

3. What activates God's strength to the weary and His power to him who lacks?

_____

_____

4. List the reasons found in Isaiah 43:1–7 why God's people should not be fearful.

_____

_____

_____

_____

5. Isaiah 66:23 and Romans 14:10–12 indicate that every person will bow down before the LORD. When will this occur?

_____

_____

6. In what manner will the redeemed of the LORD return to Zion?

_____

_____

What will they gain?

_____

_____

7. Lovely feet belong to the people who do what things?

_____

_____

_____

_____

8. Match the following excerpts from Isaiah 53 with the corresponding verses from the New Testament.

New Testament Scriptures:
Matthew 8:17, 27:29, 38, 57–60, John 12:38, Romans 4:25, 1 Peter 2:23, 1 Peter 2:24, 1 Peter 2:25

_____   A. "Who has believed our message? And to whom has the arm of the LORD been revealed?" (Isaiah 53:1).

_____   B. "He was despised and forsaken of men" (Isaiah 53:3).

_____   C. "Surely our griefs He Himself bore, and our sorrows He carried" (Isaiah 53:4).

_____   D. "He was pierced through for our transgressions, He was crushed for our iniquities" (Isaiah 53:5).

_____   E. "By His scourging we are healed" (Isaiah 53:5).

_____   F. "All of us like sheep have gone astray" (Isaiah 53:6).

_____   G. "He was oppressed and He was afflicted, yet He did not open His mouth" (Isaiah 53:7).

_____   H. "His grave was assigned with wicked men" (Isaiah 53:9).

_____   I. "He was with a rich man in His death" (Isaiah 53:9).

9. The LORD is concerned with what spending habits?

_____

_____

What are the keys to delighting in abundance?

_____

_____

10. In Luke 4:16–21, Jesus read from the beginning of Isaiah 61, saying, "Today, this Scripture has been fulfilled in your hearing." List the great things that Isaiah prophesied the Messiah ("Anointed One") would do.

_____

_____

_____

_____

11. Psalms 105 and 106 each describe an overlapping period of Israel's history to support different themes. For each of these Psalms, which period of history is covered and which theme is presented?

_____

_____

_____

_____

Unit 9 Letters to Churches in Asia Minor and Macedonia

1. What is the role of the Jewish law?

   _____

   _____

2. Explain the allegory of the two women and their sons.

   _____

   _____

   _____

   _____

3. Describe the specific responsibilities of the following:

   Wife to husband—

   _____

   _____

   Husband to wife—

   _____

   _____

   Children to parents—

   _____

   _____

Father to children—

_____

_____

4. Describe the full armor of God.

_____

_____

_____

_____

_____

Along with taking up the full armor of God, what two other things must we do?

_____

_____

5. Philippians 2:5–8 exhorts us to take on the same attitude (mindset) as Christ Jesus. To meet mankind in person, Jesus made what three specific changes to Himself?

_____

_____

_____

What was the ultimate demonstration of His attitude?

_____

_____

Therefore, what is key to our taking on the Christ mindset?

_____

_____

6. Paul planned to send Timothy to the Philippians soon after writing this letter. What were Timothy's qualifications?

_____

_____

_____

_____

7. List Paul's exhortations in Philippians 4:4–9.

_____

_____

_____

_____

8. What did Paul specifically pray for on behalf of the Colossians?

_____

_____

_____

_____

9. From Colossians 1:16–20, what are three roles of Christ Jesus?

_____

_____

_____

10. What did Paul exhort the Colossians to put on (literally, to clothe themselves with)?

_____

_____

_____

11. What are the events that will occur when Jesus returns to earth?

_____

_____

_____

How can this knowledge help us in the here and now?

_____

_____

To what is the coming of the Lord compared?

_____

_____

What is to be our response?

_____

_____

12. From 2 Thessalonians, what are the signs that will precede the return of Jesus to earth?

_____

_____

_____

_____

_____

Semester 1 Exam

1. What was the advice of the elders to Rehoboam?

    _____

    _____

    What was the advice of the young men who grew up with him?

    _____

    _____

    Whose advice did he follow?

    _____

    What were the consequences?

    _____

    _____

2. Why did the priests, Levites, and those from the tribes of Israel who were God-seekers, move from Israel to Judah and Jerusalem?

    _____

    _____

    _____

3. What was Elijah's challenge to the people at Mount Carmel?

    _____

    _____

    How did Elijah mock the prophets of Baal?

    _____

    _____

How did the LORD support Elijah?

_____

_____

_____

4. What were the first two things Jehoshaphat did when he was confronted by the Moabites, the Ammonites, and the Meunites?

_____

_____

Whom did he send out before (in front of) the army?

_____

5. What two ways will God help each of us to deal with temptation?

_____

_____

_____

6. Who were the eyewitnesses to the resurrected Jesus listed by Paul?

_____

_____

_____

_____

What does it mean if there is no resurrection of the dead (as some of the Corinthians had claimed)?

_____

_____

_____

_____

_____

7. Why was Israel ultimately deported to Assyria?

_____

_____

_____

8. From Acts 2, in his sermon on the Day of Pentecost, the Apostle Peter quoted

from Joel 2:28–32 to describe the outpouring of _____ .

9. Why were the people of Judah deported to Babylon?

_____

_____

_____

How long were they held in captivity?

_____

Who ordered their return to the land of Judah?

_____

10. Explain the meaning of the following message: "I gave you a king in My anger and took him away in My wrath (Hosea 13:11)."

_____

_____

_____

_____

11. What is to be our attitude in giving?

_____

_____

What attitudes are we to avoid?

_____

_____

12. What are we to do with each and every thought?

_____

_____

13. List the names for the Messiah found in Isaiah 7, 9, and 12.

_____

_____

_____

_____

14. In 1 Peter 2:4–8, the Apostle Peter quoted from Isaiah 28:16—Jesus Christ is

a _____ and _____ corner stone, the foundation of a spiritual house, built up with believers, who all, like Jesus,

are _____ stones.

15. What activates God's strength to the weary and His power to him who lacks?

_____

_____

16. In Luke 4:16–21, Jesus read from the beginning of Isaiah 61, saying, "Today, this Scripture has been fulfilled in your hearing." List the great things that Isaiah prophesied the Messiah ("Anointed One") would do.

_____

_____

_____

_____

_____

17. Describe the full armor of God.

_____

_____

_____

_____

_____

Along with taking up the full armor of God, what two other things must we do?

_____

_____

18. What did Paul exhort the Colossians to put on (literally, to clothe themselves with)?

_____

_____

_____

Semester 2
Activities

1. **Presentation:** Prepare a multi-chart (or computer-based) presentation on messianic prophecies. Separate the prophecies into those already fulfilled by Jesus' life and ministry and those to be fulfilled by Jesus' second coming.

2. **Drawings:** Create artistic drawings of one or more of Zechariah's apocalyptic visions.

3. **Costume:** Design a costume for the full armor of God (Ephesians 6:13–18).

4. **Photo album:** Create a photo album to describe in pictures the themes of 1 John. Take your own photos wherever possible.

5. **Report:** Is abortion ever morally and ethically acceptable? What does the Bible say directly, and indirectly, about abortion? Write a paper that describes your position and provide support. See Jeremiah 1:5, Hosea 12:3, and Luke 1:41.

Essays

1. Discuss events in Jeremiah's ministry where God sent him out to confront others. What messages did Jeremiah bring? How were his messages received? How was he treated? How did he react?

2. Describe some of the visions that God gave to Ezekiel. How did Ezekiel react to them? Which vision do you find most interesting or unusual? How do you think you would react if God showed you such a vision?

3. Describe the events surrounding the disembodied hand that appeared and wrote on the wall (Daniel 5). What does the expression "the writing on the wall" mean?

4. What were the reasons that the Jewish people were taken into captivity? What lessons did God want them to learn? After their return to their homeland, had they learned these lessons, or not? Support your answer.

5. Compare the tone and mood of the letters Paul wrote during his first imprisonment (Ephesians, Philippians, Colossians, Philemon) to the letter he wrote during his second imprisonment (2 Timothy).

6. Due to its unknown authorship, the book of Hebrews originally had difficulty being included in the New Testament. Provide detailed arguments, based upon the book's content, to support its inclusion.

7. Compare the teaching of justification by faith alone (Romans 3:21–5:21) with the teaching of faith without deeds is dead (James 2:14–26). Are these teachings complementary or conflicting? Support your answer.

8. What lessons can be learned from the messages to the seven churches in Revelation 1–3?

Unit 10 Jeremiah, Part 1

1. How does Micah 5:2, a prophecy about the birthplace of the Messiah, show that the Messiah is more than mortal?

_____

_____

2. From Nahum 1, what three offenses of the Ninevites are listed?

_____

_____

_____

3. From Habakkuk 2, how is a righteous person identified?

_____

_____

4. From Zephaniah 3:12–20, list the promises of the LORD to the remnant of Israel.

_____

_____

_____

_____

_____

5. How does Jeremiah 1:5 show the immorality of abortion?

_____

_____

_____

6. List the promises the LORD made to Jeremiah when He called him.

_____

_____

_____

_____

7. The LORD told Jeremiah to stand at the temple gate and deliver a message. What was the key theme of that message?

_____

_____

_____

How had Judah turned the temple into a "den of robbers?"

_____

_____

_____

Later on, Jesus quoted from this Scripture to support what actions on His part?

_____

_____

8. What are the proper things to boast about?

_____

_____

What are the improper things to boast about?

_____

_____

9. What was the object lesson of the pottery?

_____

_____

_____

_____

10. Jeremiah became distressed when following the LORD's instructions when mistreated by Pashhur. What did the LORD promise to do?

_____

_____

_____

_____

11. From Psalm 113, when should the name of the LORD be praised?

_____

_____

Unit 11 Jeremiah, Part 2

1. King Zedekiah sent Pashhur to Jeremiah to inquire of the LORD regarding the war against Babylon. Who did Jeremiah say, along with the king of Babylon and the Chaldeans, would war against Judah?

_____

For the people, what was the "way of life" and what was the "way of death"?

_____

_____

_____

2. The righteous Branch of David would be called by what name?

_____

_____

3. From Jeremiah 26, Jeremiah and Uriah prophesied against Jerusalem and Judah. Subsequently, each were threatened with being put to death. How did each respond to the threat? What happened to each?

_____

_____

_____

_____

4. What was Hananiah's reaction to Jeremiah's prophecy/object lesson of the wooden yoke?

_____

_____

What was the penalty for Hananiah's reaction?

_____

_____

5. The Apostle Matthew, in his gospel, quoted from Jeremiah 31:15, indicating its fulfillment by what terrible action during the early childhood of Jesus?

_____

_____

_____

6. Hebrews Chapters 8–9 quotes from Jeremiah 31:31–34 regarding God's new covenant. Who is the mediator of God's new covenant?

_____

Who are the recipients of God's new covenant?

_____

7. What was the penalty to King Jehoiakim for burning Jeremiah's scroll?

_____

_____

_____

8. When Johanan, the commanders, and all the people, asked Jeremiah to pray to the LORD for a message for them, what did they promise?

_____

_____

How long did it take for the LORD to answer Jeremiah?

_____

What was the message?

_____

_____

What was their reaction to the message?

_____

_____

_____

9. What was the LORD's purpose for instructing Jeremiah to hide some large stones at Pharaoh's palace in Tahpanhes?

_____

_____

_____

10. Psalm 119 is a great poem about God's Word. List at least seven synonyms for God's Word found there.

_____

_____

_____

Unit 12 Letters to Church Leaders and Hebrews

1. Why, in the later times, will some fall away from the faith?

_____

_____

_____

2. In the examples of the soldier, the athlete, and the farmer, what is the character trait and the goal for each?

_____

_____

_____

_____

3. What is the four-fold benefit of Scripture?

_____

_____

4. What behavior did Titus need to demonstrate, and why?

_____

_____

_____

5. From Philemon, list examples of Paul's tactfulness.

_____

_____

_____

_____

_____

_____

6. Why did the Hebrews under Moses fail to enter God's rest?

_____

_____

For believers, what is God's rest?

_____

_____

_____

7. List three examples of the potential of the Word of God.

_____

_____

_____

8. Compare the impact of the first and new covenants upon our consciences.

_____

_____

_____

_____

9. What final act will complete our salvation?

_____

_____

_____

10. Identify the person or persons for each of the following acts of faith from Hebrews 11.

_____   A. Upon his death, mentioned the exodus of the Hebrews.

_____   B. By reverence, prepared an ark for the salvation of his household.

_____   C. Considered that God is able to raise his son from the dead.

_____   D. Chose to endure ill-treatment with the people of God, rather than enjoy the passing pleasures of sin.

_____   E. Went out, not knowing where he was going.

_____   F. Obtained witness that he was pleasing to God.

_____   G. Received the ability to conceive after the proper time of life.

_____   H. Did not perish with the disobedient ones after having welcomed the spies in peace.

_____   I. Shut the mouths of lions.

_____   J. Though he is dead, he still speaks.

11. Psalm 123 provides instruction for lifting our eyes to Him who is enthroned in heaven. In what two ways are we to look to the LORD our God?

_____

_____

_____

How long do we continue?

_____

_____

Unit 13 Ezekiel

1. In Ezekiel's first vision of heaven, the LORD appeared as what figure?

    _____

    _____

    What words did the LORD use to describe the children of Israel?

    _____

    _____

2. Describe the object which the LORD told Ezekiel to eat.

    _____

    _____

    When Ezekiel ate it, how did it taste?

    _____

    _____

    What did this object symbolize and what was Ezekiel to do?

    _____

    _____

    _____

3. Who did the LORD appoint as a watchman to the house of Israel?

    _____

How was the watchman to be held accountable for his warnings?

_____

_____

_____

_____

_____

_____

_____

4. In a vision, the LORD took Ezekiel to the temple in Jerusalem. What four great abominations did he see there?

_____

_____

_____

_____

_____

_____

5. At what three places did the glory of the LORD stop on its departure out of the temple?

_____

_____

_____

6. How would the Hebrews be changed when they returned to the land of Israel after their foreign captivity?

_____

_____

_____

7. Ezekiel 12:1–16 is a prophecy about the fall of Jerusalem, which is described in 2 Kings 25:1–7. Compare these two passages.

_____

_____

_____

_____

8. In the allegory of the two eagles and the vine, what did each represent?

_____

_____

_____

9. Prior to the death of Ezekiel's wife, the LORD instructed Ezekiel that he would not be allowed to mourn publicly. This became a sign for what event and response?

_____

_____

_____

10. From Psalm 128, what are the blessings to him who fears the LORD and walks in His ways?

_____

_____

_____

Unit 14 Daniel

1. What was the main accusation from the LORD against the shepherds of Israel?

_____

_____

What were the main reasons why the LORD will judge between different sheep?

_____

_____

Who is the single shepherd the LORD will set over His flock to feed them and to be their shepherd (see also John 10:1–18)?

_____

2. Describe Ezekiel's vision of the valley of dry bones. Who did the dry bones represent?

_____

_____

_____

_____

_____

_____

3. What was the meaning of Ezekiel gripping two sticks in one hand?

_____

_____

_____

_____

4. In the prophecy against Gog, what was to happen when they attacked the land of Israel?

_____

_____

_____

_____

5. In Ezekiel's vision of the new temple, where did the glory of the LORD come from?

_____

_____

_____

Why was the east gate shut?

_____

_____

6. In Nebuchadnezzar's dream of the great statue, what object smashed the statue? What did that object represent?

_____

_____

_____

7. What happened to the soldiers who threw the three Hebrews into the blazing furnace?

_____

_____

    Who was the fourth man who joined them in the furnace?

_____

_____

8. How did Nebuchadnezzar lose his sanity?

_____

_____

    How did he regain his sanity?

_____

_____

9. What was the interpretation of the writing on the wall?

_____

_____

_____

When was this fulfilled?

_____

10. What happened to the men who schemed to get Daniel thrown into the lions' den?

_____

_____

11. From Psalm 133, to what two things is the unity of believers compared?

_____

_____

_____

Unit 15 Letters from Original Disciples and Brothers of Jesus

1. From James, what is to be our attitude toward trials?

_____

What does the testing of our faith produce?

_____

What is the blessing for the man who perseveres under trial?

_____

_____

2. What makes a person's religion worthless?

_____

_____

What is acceptable religion to God?

_____

_____

_____

3. List four examples to show that faith without good actions is useless.

_____

_____

_____

_____

_____

_____

4. List five benefits for believers who follow Christ's example in suffering.

_____

_____

_____

_____

_____

_____

5. From 2 Peter, what is more powerful than the apostle's eyewitness account of Father God's voice from heaven?

_____

_____

6. From 1 John, through which senses did John physically witness and experience the Son of God?

_____

_____

7. Why are we to walk in the Light as Father God is in the Light?

_____

_____

_____

Why are we to confess our sins?

_____

_____

_____

Why are we to abide in Jesus?

_____

_____

_____

Why are we to lay down our lives for our brothers and sisters?

_____

_____

_____

Why are we to love one another?

_____

_____

_____

8. What is the victory that has overcome the world?

_____

9. From 3 John, in what areas does John pray for prosperity?

_____

_____

What is the measure for this prosperity?

_____

10. From Jude, what topic had Jude originally planned to write about?

_____

What topic did Jude write about in its place?

_____

_____

Unit 16 Return from Exile

1. Which king did the LORD use to cause the return of the Hebrews to Jerusalem to rebuild the temple?

_____

How was the project funded?

_____

_____

What things did the king bring out to be returned to the temple?

_____

_____

2. When the foundation for the temple was laid, how did the people react?

_____

_____

How did many of the priests, Levites, and heads of households react?

_____

_____

Why?

_____

_____

3. King Artaxerxes made a decree to provide funding to Ezra for what purpose?

_____

_____

What sources were included in this funding?

_____

_____

4. Why did Ezra call a fast?

_____

_____

5. Why did Nehemiah fast and pray before the LORD?

_____

_____

How did Nehemiah get the king's attention?

_____

_____

_____

What was Nehemiah's request to the king?

_____

_____

Why did the king grant Nehemiah's request?

_____

_____

6. What strategies did Nehemiah deploy to protect the people rebuilding the wall?

_____

_____

_____

_____

_____

_____

7. When the people of Israel met together while fasting and wearing sackcloth and dirt, what did they do?

_____

_____

_____

_____

_____

8. List the key events in the book of Esther that led to the deliverance of the Jewish people from certain death.

_____

_____

_____

_____

_____

9. Why did Esther call a fast?

_____

_____

10. List some of the ironic events involving Haman.

_____

_____

_____

_____

_____

_____

11. From Psalm 139, what is the knowledge that is too wonderful and too high to be attained?

_____

_____

Where can one go to flee the LORD's presence?

_____

_____

Describe the LORD's involvement in creating each of us.

_____

_____

_____

_____

Unit 17 Transition

1. When the Hebrews failed to finish the temple rebuilding project, what kind of drought did the LORD bring upon them?

_____

_____

_____

2. The rebuilt temple survived until the destruction of Jerusalem in 70 A. D. How would the glory of that temple be greater than the previous one (of Solomon) (Haggai 2:9)?

_____

_____

_____

3. List three ways Zechariah told us to treat others.

_____

_____

_____

_____

4. What does the LORD promise to those who return to Him?

_____

_____

5. What specific details did Zechariah foretell about Jesus' triumphal entry?

_____

_____

_____

6. What specific details did Zechariah foretell about Judas' act of betrayal?

_____

_____

_____

7. What specific details did Zechariah foretell about Jesus' death on the cross that gives us cause to mourn?

_____

_____

_____

From Zechariah 13:1, what is the significance of the fountain and what does it give us cause to do?

_____

_____

_____

8. After the Last Supper, Jesus quoted from Zechariah 13:7. What was His two-fold purpose for doing so?

_____

_____

_____

9. How can a person rob the LORD?

_____

_____

How can a person test the LORD?

_____

_____

What does the LORD promise in return?

_____

_____

_____

_____

10. What prophet would appear prior to the "great and terrible day of the LORD"?

_____

What would this man do?

_____

_____

In the New Testament, who did Jesus identify as Elijah?

_____

Unit 18 Revelation

1. Describe John's vision of the Son of Man (Jesus Christ the Lord).

   _____

   _____

   _____

   _____

   What were the seven stars?

   _____

   _____

   What were the seven lamp stands?

   _____

   _____

   What were their names?

   _____

   _____

   _____

2. The Lord found no fault with which two churches?

   _____

   _____

3. What are the promises to the overcomer?

_____

_____

_____

_____

_____

_____

4. In John's vision of heaven, what do the four living creatures do continually?

_____

_____

_____

What do the twenty-four elders do in response?

_____

_____

_____

5. What event caused John to weep?

_____

_____

_____

Who told John to stop weeping?

_____

What reason did he give?

_____

_____

_____

6. With what was the great harlot drunk?

_____

_____

What is the judgment planned for her?

_____

_____

What are the reasons given from heaven for this judgment?

_____

_____

_____

7. Describe the great battle between the heavenly forces, led by the Lord Jesus, and the earthly forces, led by the beast.

_____

_____

_____

_____

8. After the thousand-year reign of Christ on earth, how large will be the army that Satan assembles?

_____

_____

Describe this last battle.

_____

_____

_____

_____

9. On Judgment Day, when all the dead will be judged, what must be true for a person to be kept from being thrown into the lake of fire?

_____

_____

_____

What things will also be thrown into the lake of fire?

_____

_____

10. Once the Judgment Day is complete, what will happen to the first heaven and earth?

_____

_____

What other "first things" will pass away as well?

_____

_____

11. Why is there no temple in the New Jerusalem city?

_____

_____

Why does the city have no sun, moon, nor lamps?

_____

_____

_____

12. Where is the tree of life located?

_____

_____

_____

Who has the right to access the tree of life?

_____

_____

Semester 2 Exam

1. From Habakkuk 2, how is a righteous person identified?

_____

_____

2. How does Jeremiah 1:5 show the immorality of abortion?

_____

_____

3. The Apostle Matthew, in his gospel, quoted from Jeremiah 31:15, indicating its fulfillment by what terrible action during the early childhood of Jesus?

_____

_____

4. Hebrews Chapters 8–9 quotes from Jeremiah 31:31–34 regarding God's new covenant. Who is the mediator of God's new covenant?

_____

   Who are the recipients of God's new covenant?

_____

5. What is the four-fold benefit of Scripture?

_____

_____

_____

6. Why did the Hebrews under Moses fail to enter God's rest?

_____

_____

    For believers, what is God's rest?

_____

_____

_____

7. How would the Hebrews be changed when they returned to the land of Israel after their foreign captivity?

_____

_____

_____

8. Prior to the death of Ezekiel's wife, the LORD instructed Ezekiel that he would not be allowed to mourn publicly. This became a sign for what event and response?

_____

_____

_____

9. Describe Ezekiel's vision of the valley of dry bones. Who did the dry bones represent?

_____

_____

_____

_____

_____

_____

10. What happened to the soldiers who threw the three Hebrews into the blazing furnace?

_____

_____

Who was the fourth man who joined them in the furnace?

_____

_____

_____

11. What makes a person's religion worthless?

_____

_____

What is acceptable religion to God?

_____

_____

_____

12. From 2 Peter, what is more powerful than the apostle's eyewitness account of Father God's voice from heaven?

_____

_____

13. What strategies did Nehemiah deploy to protect the people rebuilding the wall?

_____

_____

_____

_____

_____

14. List the key events in the book of Esther that led to the deliverance of the Jewish people from certain death.

_____

_____

_____

_____

_____

15. The rebuilt temple survived until the destruction of Jerusalem in 70 A. D. How would the glory of that temple be greater than the previous one (of Solomon) (Haggai 2:9)?

_____

_____

_____

16. What prophet would appear prior to the "great and terrible day of the LORD"?

_____

_____

What would this man do?

_____

_____

In the New Testament, who did Jesus identify as Elijah?

_____

17. In John's vision of heaven, what do the four living creatures do continually?

_____

_____

_____

What do the twenty-four elders do in response?

_____

_____

_____

_____

18. Once the Judgment Day is complete, what will happen to the first heaven and earth?

_____

_____

What other "first things" will pass away as well?

_____

_____

_____

Made in United States
Troutdale, OR
07/09/2023